IF HE LOVES ME,
WHY DOESN'T HE TELL ME?

HAL LARSON

HALO BOOKS
San Francisco, California

Published by

HALO BOOKS
Post Office Box 2529
San Francisco, CA 94126

Copyright © 1994 by Halo Books

Library of Congress Card Number
93-24300

Library of Congress-in-Publication Data

Larson, Hal, 1924-
If he loves me, why doesn't he tell me. / Hal
Larson.

p. cm.
ISBN 1-879904-11-X : $12.95
1. Love. 2. Intimacy (Psychology) 3.
Interpersonal Communication. 4. Interpersonal
Relations. I. Title.
BF575.L8L29 1994   93-24300
158'.2--dc20   CIP

Manufactured in the United States of America

for

Susie

I love you.

ACKNOWLEDGMENTS

The first supporter of the idea of this book was a remarkable man— a former cold warrior who planted seeds of love wherever he went, a Johnny Appleseed of peace and understanding.

Joe Colton understood as few people do that we are here on earth to learn, and that the most important thing we can learn is to love.

So in its small way, the book is a memorial to the generous and sunny spirit of the late Joe Colton.

My loving thanks to my wife Susan, who joined me in the months of interviews, organized and edited the transcripts, and designed the book.

And thanks to Ralph Holmstad, an early and active advocate of the book,

whose magical typewriter produced
subtly edited versions of the initial drafts.

Thanks, too, to Carole Bosch for her
omnipresent help and Diane Hume, who
shepherded the final manuscript into
print.

Finally, my profound thanks for the
kindness and patience of the hundreds of
people whose lives provided much of the
text of the book.

TABLE OF CONTENTS

PREFACE

Researching an earlier book, *Suddenly Single!,* my wife Susan and I conducted hundreds of interviews with groups and individuals who had lost a love.

We were struck by the fact that most of the losses that resulted from divorce or breakup share a single symptom. Typical comments went like this:

"He never told me he loved me."

"Never once did I hear her say 'I love you.'"

"Neither of us could talk about love."

At the heart of their problems was a common complaint: One — or both — simply never told the other "I love you."

Consider that for a moment. Is it possible that one of the single greatest causes of unhappiness on earth is failure to utter three simple words?

And could the consequences of that failure reach into the history of nations? Are the Hitlers of history the wanton product of...

But enough. We concern ourselves here with the happiness of two people. And the sermon is simple:

The lives of lovers are made more joyous by telling each other "I love you." Every day. A hundred times a day.

Tell your love "I love you" — not to prevent the heartbreak of breakup, but to bring sunshine and joy and laughter into your lives.

It is the simplest, easiest, least expensive happiness prescription there is. Think of the joy that floods your heart when your lover speaks those words to you.

Your feet leave the ground. Colors become more vivid, music more moving. You feel a sudden surge of rapture.

And your love, who spoke the words, shares your joy. As the poet said of mercy, speaking your love blesses both giver and receiver.

It is a happiness that is yours to enjoy and share every moment of your life.

And it is so easy.

If you have not told your love lately, try it.

"I love you."

See?

ABOUT THE AUTHOR

Hal Larson has written for newspapers, magazines, film and television. His first book, *Suddenly Single!*, written with his wife Susan, was published in 1989.

He has edited several books, including *You Are My Friend* and *The First Green Christmas*.

With their two young daughters, the Larsons divide their time between Mexico and the San Francisco Bay Area.

I.

"I LOVE YOU."

In all the world, there is no gift more richly satisfying and fulfilling than that sweet piece of eternity that is yours when the one you love looks into your soul and says "I love you."

Irrespective of where this happens — across a candlelit table, at a concert in the park, after an argument, holding hands on a carefree walk, while making love — it is itself a way of making love.

You treasure and remember those moments forever. You recall the place and time, the sound of his voice, the look in her eyes, how you felt, what you did — all of this is the stuff of true love.

Your heart was so engulfed that happiness spilled out of your eyes. There can be no greater gift.

Now ask yourself this: If that moment is such a wonderful gift to *receive,* why are we so reluctant to *give* it again and again and again?

What better way to give happiness to the one you love? "I love you" never wears out or becomes dated. On the contrary, it becomes richer and more rewarding with repetition.

And consider: it is a gift that enriches both the receiver and giver. It nourishes your shared love, fulfills your oneness. It is the music of angels.

If we are here on earth to grow in wisdom and love, what better affirmation could we find? Speaking truly our love puts us in harmony with the universe, at peace with our purposes.

The worst efforts of generations of songwriters have failed to diminish the magic of three simple little words: "I love you."

So why are most of us so niggardly about saying them to the one we love?

The many and varied reasons will be explored in subsequent chapters. The bottom line is that we can begin now to give the gift that rewards us both and enriches our love, the gift that continues to give long after it is spoken.

Tell her you love her at every opportunity. Tell him you love him when he first opens his eyes in the morning. Tell her you love her over coffee, after an argument, in the supermarket, in church, making love, making popcorn.

As a once-popular song counseled, "Never stop saying I love you."

Tell him you love him. Tell her you love her again and yet once more. Tell him you love him a hundred times a day.

II.

NEVER TAKE LOVE
FOR GRANTED.

Neil and Dora had been married for 14 years when Dora packed up one morning and announced that she was leaving. Neil was thunderstruck.

"I thought everything was going fine. I have a good job. The kids are doing well in school. We've got a nice house in a good neighborhood. I don't know," he said, "I just don't understand it."

Some months later, in the same county, we met Dora at a support group meeting.

"My story," she said, "is the same as many others. I saw love die a bit every day. Never once did the kids or I come ahead of Neil's job. Never did he bring us a gift. Never did he tell me he loved me.

"I'm still in my thirties. I have a life to live — and I'm not going to watch it disappear day by day."

Paul and Margaret have been together almost five years. The first two years, Paul said, were idyllic: "We just couldn't get enough of each other."

Then, gradually at first, cold silent times crept in. Words of love began to disappear. "I don't know what started it, and I'm sure Marg doesn't either. We just stopped communicating.

"One evening I heard myself say 'It's clear to me that we're history,' and after a last frigid night together I packed up and left."

Paul shook his head. "It was all so senseless. We just didn't appreciate what we had together. We let it die. Stupid, stupid, stupid."

He was silent for a moment. "If one of us had just said 'I love you...'"

Never take love for granted. It requires care and attention. And the more care it gets, the better it gets.

Love thrives on happy surprises. A no-occasion bouquet of flowers. An unexpected romantic dinner. An impulsive, improbable time and place to make love.

And love flourishes on declarations of love. It grows more assured, more confident, more giving.

Declare your love. Tell him you love him. Tell her again. And when you have done that, tell him one more time.

Never take love for granted.

III.

THE HEART'S
REASONS

Lovers do not *think* about telling their mates they love them; it is not a considered act to elicit a response.

The words tumble out, unsummoned. People say "I love you" to their loves when the heart commands.

And the heart has its reasons.

Recall again the rush of happiness when your love says "I love you." It is a shared inner glow: a stirring of the soul.

It is a sweetness we can enjoy at will, a hundred times a day, all the days of our life.

"Once, a long time ago," Ellen told us, "Henry told me he loved me. Once. And I melted. It was the best moment of my whole life. I was dizzy with happiness. But that was it. Once. And you can't live your whole life on once."

After their divorce, Ellen ran into a widowed former high school classmate, and six months later they married.

"It's a new world," she said. "We both know how important it is, how joyful it is, to say 'I love you".'

To love is to abandon defenses. Lovers are utterly vulnerable to their mates, confident that the openness will never be abused. (Well, *almost* never. Lovers are human.)

We speak our love because speaking it is an act of love, because our greatest happiness is making our lover happy, because something magical happens with the telling and the hearing, because the words are inside us demanding to be spoken.

We speak our love because we must. Because that is what love is.

Tell him you love him. Tell her you love her. Tell him again and again and yet again. Tell her again and again and then once more.

IV.
SPEAK NOW
YOUR LOVE.

Tell your love "I love you" on every occasion — whenever the impulse is there, whenever your love is there — all day, every day.

We should say "I love you" first thing in the morning, while the sand is in our eyes. We should say it in a rainstorm, when there's thunder in the skies. We should say it in bed, at breakfast, on roller-coasters, on leaving for work, on returning from work, on hearing our love's voice.

We should say "I love you" whenever our love is near, wherever our love can hear.

But there is only one time of day that is a *must*. We must *never* go to sleep without first speaking our love.

Leah, a widow in her eighties, is one of the most radiantly happy people we know. She and Bill lived a storybook romance, loved by all who knew them. He died after a long and fulfilling life.

If you could point to just one thing, we asked her, what is the single most important reason for your extraordinarily happy marriage?

"One thing? In over 50 years," she said, "we never, ever went to sleep without first saying 'I love you!'"

The sad harvest of sleeping in anger was reaped by Marie and Derek. Both successful in their professional lives, both in their mid-thirties.

"We'd get into fights over little things: what one of us had said at a party, a mix-up on where we were to meet, what one of us thought the other meant, little unimportant things.

"And then we carried that anger into bed, where you're at your most vulnerable. Our love life went south, and we were both miserable."

Marie said they just didn't know how to stop this painful deterioration. "We could hardly wait for morning, so we could get away from each other and go to our offices."

The worst part, she said, was the "terrible, endless nights. We were both hurting, but neither of us knew how to change it."

She told the group that she still feels the hurt and anger of those nights. But she knows now that a simple "I love you, Derek" could have begun the healing process.

Tell her you love her. Tell him you love him. Tell her again and again and again. Tell him again and again and yet again. Tell her *now*.

V.

WHY WE DON'T

The simple truth is that it rarely occurs to most of us to speak our love, particularly if we have been together for some time.

Our lives are taken up with the job, the kids, the mortgage, fixing the roof, preparing dinner, what we must do tomorrow: a thousand urgent workaday concerns.

We talked with Miguel on a sunny *terraza* in Mexico. Miguel, a Mexican lawyer, had married an airline stewardess from the U.S.

He spoke at length of his dismay and emptiness. She had told him she was leaving because there was no love in their marriage.

"That simply makes no sense," he said. "I was home every evening; I wasn't seeing other women. We had a good marriage for six years. Why did she leave?"

When we asked how often he told his wife he loved her, he looked puzzled.

"That wasn't necessary," he said. "Of course she had to know I loved her."

Apparently she did not.

But while a major reason most of us do not speak our love is that we just don't think about it, there are other, more complex causes.

In many respects, baby boomers comprise a watershed generation. By their independence of thought, their questioning of what had previously been accepted as fact, by their unwillingness to play follow-the-leader, they changed the course of history.

But with these changes came other, more troublesome manifestations. And perhaps the most pronounced, most hurtful of these is a fear of intimacy.

The post-World-War-II babies saw many of their parents' generation, unable to cope with wartime and postwar dislocations, dissolving their marriages in divorce court.

Reluctant to risk the same tragedy, the young boomers sought to immunize themselves. As an unhappy consequence, a sizable percentage of them became afraid to take the risk of love.

And so they became detached observers of their own "relationships." Uninvolved, safe, empty.

They invented ingenious ways to shield themselves from becoming vulnerable, unaware that numbing their emotions carries a heavy cost. Many of them converted courtship into a contest to see which person is less vulnerable.

Courting has been something of a game all through history, but the baby boomers have elevated the game to an art form.

Evidence suggests that a sizeable percentage of the now-middle-aged pig-in-the-python generation continued the "game" into "relationships" and even into marriages.

The game seems to be some form of contest wherein one never gives the other an advantage. They develop a game strategy, actually planning their moves to keep the other on the defensive.

To speak your love, these troubled lovers think, is to weaken your bargaining position, to put your partner "one-up." And that gives the partner leverage.

Thus the historic minuet of courtship becomes a duel, with neither partner willing to concede a point to the other.

Love has a difficult time surviving in the rocky terrain of warfare. It sometimes emerges for a while as an armed truce. But to flourish, love needs to be free and unstructured.

The song of love is rarely heard above the din of battle.

It is also true that many of the baby boomers' parents refrained from speaking their love because they were taught from childhood to hide their emotions.

Much of this recalcitrance is attributable to the puritan tradition and "old-country ways," which taught that men, particularly, never displayed emotion or affection, even in private — that it would somehow diminish their manhood. And the "real men don't cry" syndrome has caused more than its share of marital mischief.

Emotional sterility may have its place on the battleground or in the boardroom, but not at the family breakfast or in the conjugal bed.

Annette and Jim married three years after the end of World War II. When the last of their three children had left the nest, Annette announced that she was leaving, too.

"I put up with it for the kids' sake," she told us. "But I couldn't live any longer with an iceberg. Do you know: Not once in more than 30 years did he tell me he loved me.

"My life isn't perfect now, but at least I'm not living on false hope. I don't lie awake nights feeling empty."

Tell her you love her. Tell him you love him. Then tell her again and yet again. Never stop saying "I love you."

VI.
THE MYTH OF
"SAFE" LANGUAGE

The trauma of parental divorce has been a major player in the reluctance of today's young — and middle-aged — to allow themselves to become vulnerable.

Before World War II, divorce was rare. The surge began during the war and increased by 1965 to 2.5 per thousand population. Divorce was reshaping the traditional family structure — and the psyche of generations.

In the next 10 years, the divorce rate almost doubled again, to 4.8 per thousand. Through the late 1970s and all of the 1980s, more than a million households per year were coming apart. Today, half of all marriages end in divorce. The emotional scar tissue on the children of these broken homes is a constant reminder not to do or say things that could come back and hurt.

Children of single parents often feel cheated of an important part of growing up: their birthright of a two-parent family. And the deeper the feeling, the greater the reluctance to risk making the same mistake their parents did.

Many children of broken homes have great difficulty sorting through their feelings. A need for stability sometimes prompts a rush into premature marriage that ends disastrously and adds to the emotional damage. Others simply develop protective machinery to guard them from the pain they felt as children.

Not having lived in a happy household, they fear they "inherit" the tendency for breakup. Many doubt they know how to behave in a loving home because they have no first-hand experience.

The effect of all this on the children of broken homes is changing the way young people feel about intimacy and permanence. A large percentage is convinced at the beginning that the romance won't last. And so they "protect" themselves.

They use "safe" language as they use safe sex: protecting themselves from unwanted consequences.

Such "safe" words as "relationship," "having sex," and "roommate" will be explored in the next two chapters.

But unlike safe sex, safe language — the language of avoidance, of non-commitment — can keep couples from genuine intimacy. It becomes a permanent barrier: what the poet Shelley called "a shroud of words to shield us from the sun of this too-familiar life."

Self-examination of our own language of love can be instructive. Do we verbally keep our arms folded on our chest to create distance? Or do we truly speak what we feel?

Although it may take effort and serious introspection, the latter is the way of happiness. Say what you feel. If you love her, *tell* her you love her. If you love him, *tell* him you love him.

Tell him again and again. Tell her again and yet again.

VII.
THE PROBLEM
WITH
"RELATIONSHIPS"

Research for the book *Suddenly Single!* yielded another unexpected finding: Among those whose loss resulted from causes other than death, a large majority referred to a breakup of a "relationship." Even formerly married people used this term.

Consider the significance of this. If what two people have together is no more than a "relationship," they have something that is imperiled from the beginning by its very label.

The word is neutral. It is devoid of the strength and tradition of "marriage," and it has none of the joy and passion of "love" or "lover" or even "love affair." These words have color and texture. "Relationship" is gray and flat.

"Relationship" implies a reluctance to commit. It is a holding pattern, not a destination. Love is forever.
"Relationship" may be blown away by the next breeze. Love has roots and grows.
"Relationship" just lies there, rootless, incapable of growth or nourishment.

Love is a two-way street.
"Relationship" is a parking lot.

For those students of semantics who would remind us that the word is not the thing, we point out that over time interpersonal things can be circumscribed and diminished by the word. Children who are repeatedly told they are "ugly" or "dumb" or "unwanted" carry a lasting scar.

When partners habitually refer to themselves as being in, or having, a "relationship," they are declaring that this is something less than love. Otherwise, why the longer, non-specific, colorless term?

To be in love is to be like Robert Louis Stevenson's fully-exposed cow: "tossed by all the winds that blow and wet with all the showers." It is total immersion, unguarded rapture, unqualified vulnerability.

And it is perhaps in that word "vulnerability" that the explanation for "relationship" lies. "Relationship" suggests that what the couple feels is tentative, unsure, lacking commitment. It means they are unwilling to accept the vulnerability that is an essential ingredient of love.

Wendy lived with Dave for three years. When the "relationship" ended, she put it like this:

"I guess both of us were playing our cards close to our vests. I thought that to come out and say what I felt, that I really loved Dave, would have put me at a disadvantage. He would have had all the leverage. And now, in retrospect, I think he felt the same way.

"I don't exactly know why, but both of us were guarded about what we said. And that's the way it ended. He walked out without a word."

If they could have been less defensive, less cautious, they would likely still be enjoying a lovely and enriching love affair. And, probably, marriage.

Like pregnancy, perfection and death, love cannot be qualified. You love or you do not love. And like all living things, love needs nourishment.

A joyful way to nourish your love is to speak your love. Tell her you love her. Tell him you love him. Then tell your love again, and yet again.

VIII.
OTHER
TIP-OFF TERMS

How couples speak of their togetherness provides clues to the stability of their romance.

Most of those we spoke with who had experienced breakup tended to talk of "having sex," rather than "making love."

"Having sex" has all the joy and warmth of having measles. It is impersonal, cold and remote. Instead of evoking the joy of love, it suggests an activity as pleasurable and as passionate as paying taxes.

Conversely, "making love" speaks to the shared giving and mutual rapture of the deepest, truest expression of loving.

The one comes off the shelf; the other from the heart.

Similarly, terms used to describe the person we love can foretell the depth of commitment and staying power of the romance.

"Roommate," "friend," and the terminally cute "significant other" all say nothing of being in love, of sharing a joyful commitment to each other. In fact, the words themselves create emotional distance.

Duane, a heartbroken man in his mid-twenties, was at a total loss to understand what went wrong. After all, he told us, he and his "roommate" had "sex" with some regularity. Speaking with us, he never once used the word "love."

Duane's "roommate" moved out one morning with a casual "See ya."

Listen to the language of your friends.
How do they refer to each other and what
they do alone together? Do they use the
distant, impersonal words of people in a
"relationship?"

Or do they speak the language of
those truly in love, who introduce their
mates with obvious pride: "This is my
wife." "This is my love."?

You can be reasonably certain which
has the depth to flourish and grow.

Glory in your love. It is the best part
of living. Tell him you love him in the
morning when he's shaving. Tell her you
love her when she's had a tough day.

Then tell him again. Tell her once
more. And tell him again. Tell her again
and yet again.

IX.
START SMALL.

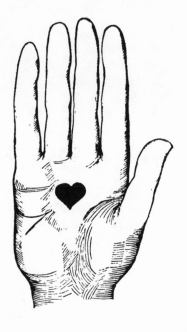

"To be honest, there are a lot of times I *want* to tell her I love her. But we've gotten into a kind of rut, I guess. And we always somehow end up in an argument."

Mark was an engineer for a large company. He and Angie had been married seven years. But both felt it was a failure. They talked of divorce.

Their counselor saw reason for hope and suggested a simple strategy. "Every time you feel like criticizing, stop yourself and find something positive to say. It doesn't have to be much:

"'Good soup.' 'That looks nice on you.' 'Happy anniversary.' "How about taking a walk?' 'I like your hair like that.'"

Somewhat haltingly, they tried. Insults gave way to compliments. Arguments continued, but were no longer vicious. They began *looking* for good things to say about each other.

"It's a different marriage now," Angie told us. "We begin and end each day with 'I love you' and we've discovered that we really *do* love each other."

Mark and Angie found out before it was too late. Many couples don't. Old habits die hard.

"I really know we loved each other," said Grace, "but we let ourselves slide into a pattern of cold silence. We just couldn't get the words out.'

"The silence became a weight on us; something had to give. I did. I got up in the middle of the night and left. I left everything I owned."

Her story did not end happily, nor did those of scores of others we interviewed. Many said they did not speak their love because they were afraid of having it backfire.

"I was concerned that Wayne would throw it back in my face if I said I loved him," Barbara told us, "and now I have the distance to believe he felt the same way. Why couldn't we understand what we had? Why do we hide what we feel?"

The mounting pressure ended explosively. They had a bruising fight and a costly court battle.

The advice that helped save the marriage of Mark and Angie could have been useful to Grace and to Barbara and Wayne and to many others: Start small. Find little compliments and substitute them for criticism. Look for good things to say.

"I love you" will follow as naturally as night follows day. And "I love you" brings light and laughter and love into the dark corners of life.

Tell her you love her. Tell him you love him. Tell her again and again and yet again. Then tell him you love him once more.

X.

"I LOVE YOU, DAD."

Bookshelves overflow with autobiographical novels and learned disquisitions about the special problems of communicating with fathers.

Sons, especially, write of their anguish over the fact that they were never able to say "I love you, Dad." And, equally, they grieve because Pop never told them.

Few feelings are stronger — or less understood — than the bond between father and son. Psychologists say there is a palpable hunger for sons to feel that they are valued by their fathers.

After a two-hour sensitivity session with business executives at the Menninger clinic in Wichita, Kansas, the attending psychologist pointed out that while all the participants had spoken of a deep yearning for the approbation of their fathers, not one had mentioned his mother.

Most adult males will immediately recognize themselves in this truism: man spends most of his life trying to prove himself to his father.

Long after the death of the father, the son continues to seek his approval. Roots of this run deep.

But altogether too often, these intense feelings are not communicated by either father or son. Frequently they mask their message in familiar activities: "We always played catch instead of talking, but we both understood."

But *did* they? More than likely, the

substitute activity was a convenient form of avoidance and only added to the angst. These evasions tend to assure the ache that comes when it is too late: after there's no father to tell.

In his autobiography, Dwight Eisenhower wrote "My only regret is that it was always so difficult to let my father know the great depth of my affection for him."

No one fully understands the unique communications problem between fathers and sons. Some professional therapists have suggested that the problem arises from the unreachable depth of the feelings. But that does little to resolve the dilemma.

And the distance between father and son is even widening in the Political Correctness of the 90s. Many of today's mothers discourage greater paternal involvement in raising children. Several studies have found that more than half of the mothers surveyed felt diminished or threatened by Dad's participation.

Movies and TV have more than a little responsibility for deepening the wedge between father and child. If Dad isn't portrayed as an unfeeling monster, he is likely to be an incompetent bumbler.

It is difficult for youngsters not to come away from the daily barrage of media messages without some sense that Pop is superfluous.

But strong or weak, man or mouse, fathers haunt their male progeny. With all his flaws, real or imagined, Dad is a daunting figure to the son.

When the words are left unspoken between father and son, there is an ache that won't go away, a lump that stays in the throat.

The real solution is to stop agonizing about why, and tell him *now* that you love him. *Now.* Tomorrow or next week may be too late. It is helpful to remember that fathers were once sons, and emotional distance can be closed.

It would be a mistake to assume that this problem with fathers is confined to *sons.* While most literature focuses on the traumas of the male offspring, it is true that daughters have much the same dilemma with Dad.

"Dad was so formidable," Eleanor said, "I think I was intimidated by him. Even when I grew older, I was too frightened to tell him I loved him. It just never happened. I think about that a lot now. And now it's just too damned late." She couldn't hold back the tears.

The rest of your life is a long time to carry the ache of regret.

Tell him *now.* "I love you, Dad."

XI.
MOTHERS,
BROTHERS AND
OTHERS

Although the lens of literature focuses on the problems of communicating with *fathers*, others in the family have been experiencing similar difficulties since the age of Oedipus.

Mothers and daughters are likely to have much the same problem as fathers and sons — and for many of the same reasons.

Grown siblings frequently become tongue-tied when trying to express their love for each other. "How are you doing, Sis?" does not get the job done when one really means "I want you to know I love you."

How often have we heard it: "If only I had told Mom how much I loved her." Or

"My brother was a wonderful person; how I wish I had let him know how much I loved him."

We say things like that when it is too late.

But now, today, it is not too late to tell someone that you love her; not too late to say "Mom, I want you to know I love you." It is not too late to tell your brother or sister of your love.

Francine, a successful businesswoman in her forties, had lost a brother to AIDS six years before we spoke with her.

"Dad called us Pat and Mike when we were kids," she said. " We were close in age and inseparable through our growing years. Then I got involved with my business and we drifted apart. Even when I found out he was dying, I didn't tell him how much I loved him. I'll live with that the rest of my life."

As Mark Twain said about telling the truth, speaking your love may surprise some people. But it will bring joy to both you and the recipient of your love — and it can spare you an eternity of wishing you had.

And almost always, things become better after you speak your love. It is not altogether unlikely that the other person has been wanting to speak his love, too. You have done the heavy lifting, and the recipient can accept the gift with joy and relief.

It is as though a large barrier has been removed. Now you can talk of sweet, half-remembered times that, in the telling, make life richer and more worthwhile.

Tell him you love him. Tell her you love her. See if the sun doesn't become brighter, the load lighter. Tell him again. Then tell her yet again.

XII.
TELL THE
LITTLE CHILDREN.

Communication problems between parent and child begin early. Busy parents have other things on their minds, and words of love often just don't get spoken.

When children are very young, they are too busy discovering the world around them to notice. Magical things are everywhere, and the words unspoken are not missed. Yet.

But before very long, the chasm widens. The child knows something important is missing. There are times when the child hungers for the parent's love, times when "I love you" would make everything all right again. After a frightening dream, for example; when the child has broken something valuable, or become injured or misbehaved. The child desperately needs love and reassurance.

Silence begets silence. When the parent fails to speak love to the child, the child learns to reciprocate. And the pattern becomes self-reflexive. The parent, sensing rejection, becomes yet more distant, and the bewildered child bottles up his feelings and his hurt.

Later they both ache and wonder what went wrong. Later their worlds are full of "If only ..."

Guido and his wife were divorced a year after the birth of their daughter. Father and daughter went their separate ways — and the distance between them increased with time.

"I never didn't love her," he said. "I just didn't think it was necessary to say it."

One day, he wrote his daughter a long loving letter telling her how much he loved her and admired the woman she had become.

"She called me when she got the letter," he said. "She told me she loved me, too, and will keep and treasure my letter. It was an important and meaningful breakthrough for both of us."

The good news is that it is *not* too late for most people. If you've never told your child how much you love her, now is the time to start. "I love you, son." "I love you, little girl."

If it has been a long time since you

spoke those words, or if it has never happened before, you will feel a huge weight lifting from your shoulders. In that twinkling, you will know an unprecedented joy.

And the look you get from your child will go in your memory bank of life's sweetest moments.

You have not only averted a possible life-long problem; you have also given your child and you a priceless gift.

Tell your child now. "I love you, my daughter." "I love you, my son."

XIII.
SHOW YOUR LOVE.

Communicating your love is of course not an exclusively verbal pleasure. We can show our love in hundreds of joyful and inventive ways.

We do it with flowers and gifts, with a glance, by the way we touch, smile, remember little things, anticipate each other, help each other, listen, speak of our love to others, give happy surprises.

Endless are the ways we can recharge our love with happy surprises.

"I love you" lipsticked on the bathroom mirror in the morning. A love note under the grapefruit in the fridge.

A mid-morning phone call suggesting mid-day lovemaking.

Warming the other side of a cold bed before your love gets there.

Taking the kids for a walk to give your love a break.

Packing a surprise picnic lunch for a lazy summer day.

Tucking a love note into a pocket, purse, lunch box, book, briefcase.

A bubble bath for two. A massage with scented oils.

A weekend at the site of your first romantic getaway. A day at a spa.

Having your love's favorite photo enlarged and framed.

A surprise party, just to show your love.

And the way you talk *about* your loved

one. The way you beam and brag in conversation with others.

"One of the most endearing things about Mike," said Brenda, "is the way he lights up when he talks about me. He just glows. He couldn't show his love in a nicer way."

The list of ways to show our love could reach to the moon. Ways that add juice and joy to our lives.

Joyful as they are, however, they are not alternatives to speaking your love. They are sweet and happy and important. But they do not replace "I love you."

So show your love in all the endearing and imaginative ways you can think of.

But also *tell* her you love her. *Tell* him you love him. Again and again and again.

XIV.

FOR LOVERS ONLY

The recommendation to tell your lover "I love you" is meant for people who truly love.

As we all know, there are those who are simply in love with love. Many of these people confuse this non-specific yearning with true love and try to fit someone into their longing.

This is romanticism, not love. Speaking love to the unsuspecting object of your fantasy is akin to professing love to a tree. There is scant likelihood that our adoration will be reciprocated. Writing love letters to celebrities can be satisfying, but it is not love.

Couples often live together for economic reasons. This sometimes leads to love, but until and unless it does, we would be well counseled to accept the situation for just what it is and not speak the language of love to financial partner.

Infatuations, too, can become a problem if we rush pell-mell into protestations of undying love to someone who has no idea what we're talking about.

No, the language of love is for lovers only. It finds meaning in the nurturing warmth of shared giving that is love.

But if it *is* love, it becomes magical and musical and luminous when it is spoken.

Tell him you love him. Tell her you love her. Tell her again and again and yet once more.

XV.
THE WORDS
AS WEAPONS

The scene is familiar. They have had a drink, dinner, wine. He reaches across the table, takes her hand in his and breathes "I love you."

In fact, he scarcely knows her. And love has nothing to do with the evening. What he wants to do is take her to bed.

Later that night, she, too, whispers "I love you."

But like him, she is using the words as a means to an end. She wants an end to the pick-up bars and lonely nights. She wants the security of marriage.

Both are engaging in a cynical deception. Both are using "I love you" as a weapon to achieve a goal.

It could, of course, be reversed. She

could have used the words to seduce him, and he could have said them to further the ends of an economically desirable marriage.

In either case, it is profane: a crime against love. Indeed, it is blasphemy. If God is love, it is using His name in vain. Few acts are more reprehensible.

Love is a holy thing. "I love you" is a sacred connection between lovers. "I love you" is pure and clean. It is a chunk of eternity: the stuff of rainbows, the murmur of angels.

Do not speak love as a weapon. If you love her, tell her you love her. If you love him, tell him you love him in love and joy and wonder. Tell her again and yet once more.

XVI.
TOO MUCH LOVE?

The question must be asked: Can saying "I love you" be overdone?

It is possible, of course. If it becomes an endless, scratchy broken record, it is an irritant, not a song of love.

But we speak here of saying and *meaning* "I love you." And in the real world, we cannot say or hear it too often.

Spoken in love, the words will heal, bond, gladden, unify, stimulate, soar. Can anyone have too much of that?

Nora, whose joyful marriage to Joel began three years after she ended an earlier pain-filled marriage, told us that "I love you" now begins and ends every talk together.

"I didn't think I could ever be this happy," she said.

"We wake up and go to sleep with love. Joel leaves notes around our apartment that say 'I love you.' I phone him just to tell him I love and miss him. Some of our friends say they think we're crazy — but I think they really envy us."

It is likely that hundreds of thousands of loves have perished for *want* of the words. There is no recorded instance in which they were the *cause* of the death of love.

XVII.

"WORDS SPOIL THINGS."

Sages since the beginning of recorded history have taught us that words can spoil things.

Only a fool would argue that the ancient wisdom is wrong. The soundness and security of silence have been proclaimed by scholars, philosophers and virtually every religion. Words spoil things.

Generally.

The radiant exception that validates this time-honored rule is telling your love "I love you."

Instead of spoiling, it enhances, enriches, illuminates, augments. It adds music and mirth and magic.

Some lawyers and other overly-
cautious people may take issue. One
barrister recommended that you never
write what can be spoken, and never speak
what can be expressed by a nod of the
head. Perhaps so. But wisdom and
experience proclaim the luminous
rightness of giving voice to our love.

In fact, when it comes to love, it can
be truly said that *silence* can spoil things.
In the face of love, silence can be deadly.
When you love, the words demand to be
spoken.

Silence can give the lie to love, can
turn it away.

Heed the counsel of the seers — in all
things but love. When you love, let the

words find their voice. The heart knows best.

Tell him you love him. Tell her you love her. Tell him a hundred times, then tell him again. Tell her a hundred times and then once again.

XVIII.
ONCE MORE
WITH FEELING

What's all this fuss about telling your love "I love you"?

The world is experiencing wars, famines, starvation, hatreds, suffering; there is still no cure for cancer or AIDS. What's the big deal about three little words?

Precisely that. You are not being urged here to put an end to wars and pestilence or find a cure for cancer or spend a lot of money. Rather, it is being suggested that you can make one small corner of the world a better place with very little effort. You can begin doing it immediately. It takes no special skill or equipment. It costs nothing. You can do it wherever you are.

Yet for this very small effort, the

rewards are great indeed. The bond between you and your loved one becomes more joyous and secure. The moment and the day brighten. Aggravations subside.

Beyond that, a tone has been set. It is unlikely that "I love you" will be followed by nagging or complaining. Love begets love. Words of love inspire acts of love and joy.

Telling your love "I love you" is not an alternative to professional therapy. But if it is said often and with feeling, it can help create an environment that will never require therapy.

Note, too, that a growing body of medical evidence is suggesting a connection between health and happiness.

Norman Cousins and others have documented cases where love and laughter have dramatically altered the course of cancer.

Psychologists and historians have postulated for years that the true genesis of countless wars is nothing more than an extension of the unhappiness and frustration of one or two individuals. People at peace with themselves don't start wars.

However, it is not for all mankind that we suggest you speak your love. It is for you and your love. If it does no more than create a moment of joy for the two of you, is it not worth the effort?

And it could be the beginning of a lifetime of happiness.

Tell her you love her. Tell him you love him. As we reach the end of this book, this very moment could be a good time to start a new chapter in your own love story.

It is this simple: "I love you."

Tell him you love him.

Tell her you love her.

Now?

Order Form

Use this form to order additional copies of
If He Loves Me, Why Doesn't He Tell Me?
and other Halo Books.

To: Halo Books
       Post Office Box 2529
       San Francisco, CA 94126

Please send

_____   copies of **If He Loves Me** $12.95 per copy
       Why Doesn't He Tell Me?

_____   copies of **Suddenly Single!** $13.95 per copy
       A Lifeline For Anyone Who
       Has Lost A Love

_____   copies of **You Are My Friend.** $9.95 per copy
       A Celebration of Friendship

_____   copies of **Loving Children.** $9.95 per copy
       Words Of Love About Kids
       From Those Who Cherish Them

_____   copies of **Am I A Hindu?** $14.95 per copy
       The Hinduism Primer

_____   copies of **Your Sexual Health.** $15.95 per copy
       What Teenagers Need To Know
       About Sexually Transmitted
       Diseases

_____   copies of **Teenage Survival** $9.95 per copy
       Manual. *Being In Charge Of*
       Your Mind And Body In An
       Adult World

Please enclose check or money order. Add $1 shipping for one book and 50¢ for each additional book. In California please add 7% sales tax.